OUR EARTH IN ACTION

WEATHER

Chris Oxlade

FRANKLIN WATTS

LONDON•SYDNEY

First published in 2009 by Franklin Watts

Copyright © 2009 Franklin Watts

Franklin Watts
338 Euston Road
London NW1 3BH

Franklin Watts Australia
Level 17/207 Kent Street
Sydney, NSW 2000

A CIP catalogue record for this book is available
from the British Library.

Dewey number: 551.5

ISBN 978 0 7496 9026 7

Printed in China

Franklin Watts is a division of Hachette Children's Books,
an Hachette UK company.

www.hachette.co.uk

Artwork: John Alston
Editor: Sarah Ridley
Design: Thomas Keenes
Editor in Chief: John C. Miles
Art director: Jonathan Hair
Picture research: Diana Morris

Picture credits: Andriano/Shutterstock: front cover, 1. Bill Bachman/Alamy: 23.
Tibor Bognar/Corbis: 27b. Martin Bond/SPL: 21. Brasilz/Istockphoto: 28.
Andrew Burns/Shutterstock: 6. Ashey Cooper/Corbis: 29. Cubolmages srl/Alamy:
20. Tad Denson/Shutterstock: 15. Asif Hassan/Getty Images: 19. Jeanne
Hatch/Shutterstock: 4. iNNOCENt/Shutterstock: 24. Eric Joltz/Istockphoto: 27t.
Sebstian Knight/Shutterstock: 7. R McGurk/Istockphoto: 9. NASA: 13. NOAA: 14.
rotofrank/Istockphoto: 18. Lowell Sannes/Shutterstock: 16t. Colin Shepherd/Rex
Features: 16b. Paul A Souders/Corbis: 11. Kim Steele/Alamy: 22. Kim Pin
Tan/Shutterstock: 10. Drazen Vukelic/Shutterstock: 8. Kennan Ward/Corbis: 26.
Victor Leonidovich Zastolisky/Shutterstock: 5, 17. *Every attempt has been made to
clear copyright. Should there be any inadvertent omission please apply to the
publisher for rectification.*

CONTENTS

ABOUT THE WEATHER

The weather is simply a description of the conditions in the air around us and in the Earth's atmosphere, and how it changes from one day to the next. It includes how hot or cold the air is, whether the air is moving (causing winds), whether rain or snow is falling, whether the Sun is shining, and what type of clouds are in the sky.

WEATHER AND OUR LIVES

Weather plays a large part in our lives. Every day we make decisions because of the weather, such as what to wear to go outside, whether to go on a trip or play in the park. More long-term, the weather dictates how we build our homes to make them comfortable in different weather conditions, and how much energy we use. The weather is more important for certain groups of people, including farmers, who plan their crops around the weather, and sailors, who rely on winds to move their boats. The weather can be fascinating to observe, especially extreme weather events — giant hailstorms or spectacular thunderstorms — and is a popular topic of conversation. But the weather can also be dangerous: events such as hurricanes, floods and droughts have killed millions of people over the centuries. The weather affects our lives, but it is also true that our lives are affecting the weather. Our use of fossil fuels and other activities are adding gases to the atmosphere, causing changes in the weather called climate change.

▶ *Water is constantly moving between the atmosphere, the oceans and the land.*

▶ *Farmers need rain to help their crops grow but they need dry weather at harvest time.*

WORKING THE WEATHER

The weather happens in the Earth's atmosphere. It is caused by the movement of air and water around the atmosphere. The movement is driven by heat from the Sun. This warms the Earth more in some places than others, making air swirl about, creating effects from gentle breezes to vast, violent storms. It also causes weather cycles, such as the seasons that happen around the world.

The science of weather

The science of weather is called meteorology, and the scientists who study it are called meteorologists. The processes that cause weather are very complicated. Meteorologists are always trying to understand them better. They also record the weather, forecast future weather and study climate change.

EARTH'S ATMOSPHERE

The weather happens in the Earth's atmosphere — the layer of air that surrounds the planet. For example, the movement of air in the atmosphere creates winds, the movement of water in the atmosphere creates clouds and rain, and the temperature of the air in the atmosphere makes the weather hot, warm, cool or cold.

LAYERS OF THE ATMOSPHERE

The atmosphere is very thin compared to the size of the Earth. If you imagine the Earth as a balloon, the atmosphere would be about the thickness of the balloon's rubber. The air gradually thins out as altitude (height above sea level) increases. It eventually fades away into space about 200 km up. The temperature of the air changes as height increases too, but not evenly — it goes up and down. Scientists divide the atmosphere into five layers because of the way air temperature rises

▲ Jet airliners cruise above the weather, which happens in the lowest part of the atmosphere.

◀ The layers of the Earth's atmosphere. The exosphere fades away into space above 200 km.

200 km
thermopause

80 km
mesopause

50 km
stratopause

10 km
tropopause

exosphere

thermosphere

mesosphere

stratosphere

troposphere

Gases of the atmosphere

The air is a mixture of different gases. It is mostly nitrogen (about three-quarters) and oxygen (about one-fifth). Other gases make up just 1% of the atmosphere, but some are important in the weather. They include carbon dioxide, which is mainly responsible for the greenhouse effect (see page 28). There is always some water vapour in the air, which is responsible for clouds and rain.

or falls in them. The bottom layer is called the troposphere, and it is about 10 km thick. This is where almost all our weather happens. In the troposphere, the temperature falls by 7° Celsius each kilometre further up towards space. The layer above the troposphere is the stratosphere. This contains the ozone layer — a layer with a high concentration of ozone gas, which blocks out harmful ultraviolet radiation from the Sun.

AIR PRESSURE

The air is made up of billions of particles of gas, called molecules, moving at high speed. They are constantly bouncing off things in the air, and this causes a push called air pressure, or atmospheric pressure. Because the air gets thinner as you move up through the atmosphere, air pressure reduces with altitude, too. We measure air pressure in units called hectopascals (also known as millibars), using an instrument called a barometer. At sea level, atmospheric pressure is normally around 1,000 hectopascals.

▶ A barometer records changes in air pressure.

AIR PRESSURE AND WINDS

All winds, from light breezes to howling gales, are simply air moving about in the atmosphere. The air moves because of differences in air pressure from one place to another. These pressure differences happen because the Sun heats the Earth's surface in an uneven way.

CHANGING PRESSURE

When air is warmed up it expands and becomes less dense. It floats up through cooler, more dense air around it (you can see this happening on a small scale when air heated by a bonfire floats upwards, carrying smoke with it). Because the warm air expands, its pressure falls. The warm air does not keep rising forever. As it rises, it cools again, becomes more dense, and sinks back down to the surface. Its pressure also rises. Air always moves from an area of higher pressure to an area of lower pressure, so winds blow from areas where pressure is high to areas where pressure is low.

Measuring winds

Winds have both strength and direction, so we have to measure both of these to record a wind. Wind strength is measured in kilometres per hour (km/h). Wind direction is described using the points of a compass. The point shows where the wind is blowing from (for example, a westerly wind blows from the west). Wind strength is measured with an anemometer and wind direction with a wind vane.

▶ A cup anemometer (right) and a wind vane (left).

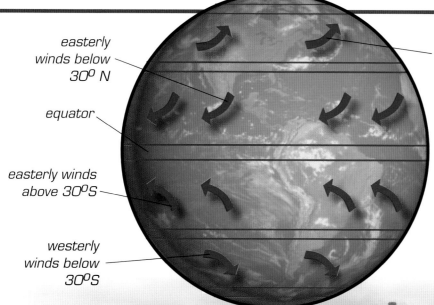

easterly winds below 30° N

westerly winds above 30°N

equator

easterly winds above 30°S

westerly winds below 30°S

◀ A diagram showing global wind patterns. In the past, all sailors had to use these patterns to cross the oceans as they relied on sails.

WIND PATTERNS

Differences in air pressure cause winds both on a local scale and on a global scale. An example of a local wind is a sea breeze. On a hot day by the sea, the land heats up quickly, but the sea does not. Air over the land warms and rises, creating low pressure. This draws in cooler air from over the sea. Global winds happen because the Earth's equatorial regions receive more heat from the Sun than the polar regions. For example, warm air over the tropics rises, and air flows in to replace it, causing winds that blow towards the equator from the north and south. The Earth's spin makes the winds curve east or west — this is called the Coriolis Effect.

▲ This flag warns swimmers of dangerous currents. The way that it is blowing shows there is a stiff sea breeze, caused by the warm land and the cool sea.

DANGER
BEYOND THIS POINT
NO SWIMMING
DUE TO OCEAN CONDITION

CLOUDS AND RAIN

The air always contains some water vapour (the gas form of water). When air cools, some of the water vapour condenses, turning from gas to liquid. It forms droplets of water or ice crystals. When billions of water droplets or ice crystals form together, they make up clouds. Eventually, the water droplets or ice crystals will fall as rain or snow.

CLOUD TYPES

Clouds form when air containing water vapour rises upwards, which makes it cooler. This can happen when air warmed over land rises, when air rises upwards in weather fronts (see page 12), or when winds blow up and over mountains. We see a wide range of different cloud forms in the sky. Meteorologists name clouds by shape and height. There are two main groups of clouds — stratus, or layered clouds, and cumulus, or heaped clouds. In addition, some cloud names include the words cirrus (high-level) and alto (middle-level). For example, cirrus clouds are high-level wispy clouds, altostratus clouds are middle-level layered clouds, and cumulus are low-level heaped clouds.

▼ These are cumulus clouds, formed by humid air rising over hot land.

PRECIPITATION

Any water or ice that falls from the sky (such as rain, snow and hail) is known as precipitation. When clouds first form, their water droplets or ice crystals are very tiny — perhaps only a few hundredths of a millimetre across. They are so light that they stay in the air because of air currents in the clouds. But when they grow big enough they fall downwards. In low-level clouds tiny droplets of water join to make larger drops, up to 2 mm across, which form rain. In middle-level and high-level clouds, tiny ice crystals grow larger until they fall as snow, although this normally melts as it falls through warmer air below. Rainfall is measured by the depth of water that gathers on the ground, in millimetres, using an instrument called a rain gauge.

▲ Stratus clouds seen above a dramatic mountain landscape.

The water cycle

Water is constantly moving between the oceans, the atmosphere and the land. This circulation is known as the water cycle. Water vapour in the atmosphere comes from evaporation of seawater and water in the soil. This falls to the surface when it turns into rain or snow (precipitation). Some flows back to the oceans along streams and rivers, and some re-evaporates into the air.

▶ A diagram of the water cycle. Rivers carry water from the land to the sea.

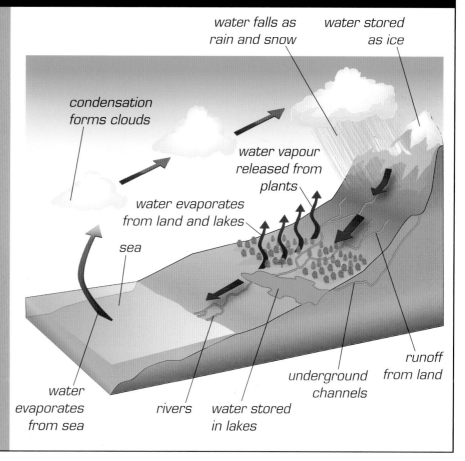

water falls as rain and snow

water stored as ice

condensation forms clouds

water vapour released from plants

water evaporates from land and lakes

sea

water evaporates from sea

rivers

water stored in lakes

underground channels

runoff from land

WEATHER FRONTS AND SYSTEMS

Because the Sun heats the Earth's surface in an uneven way, and the surface heats the air above, blocks of air with different temperatures are formed. The blocks are called air masses. A lot of the Earth's weather happens where these air masses meet each other.

WEATHER FRONTS

A weather front is the border between one air mass and another. It forms when one air mass moves into the space occupied by another. There are three main types of weather front, called warm fronts, cold fronts and occluded fronts. Each brings characteristic weather when it passes by a place. A warm front forms when a warm air mass moves into a cold air mass. Water vapour in the warm air creates high-level clouds, followed by widespread rain-bearing stratus clouds. A cold front forms when a cold air mass moves into a warm mass. This creates a band of stormy cumulus clouds along the front, and low pressure that leads to strong winds. An occluded front forms when a cold front catches up with a warm front.

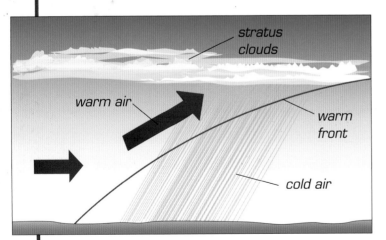

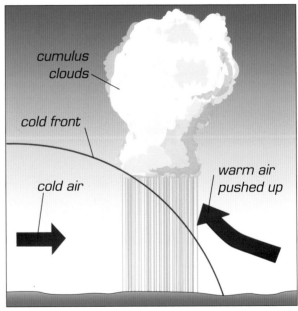

▲ At a warm front, the less dense warm air lifts over the more dense cold air. Water vapour in the slowly rising warm air creates stratus clouds.

▲ At a cold front, the more dense cold air pushes under the less dense warm air. The quickly rising warm air creates dense cumulus clouds.

SWIRLING FRONTS

Sometimes the interaction between a huge warm air mass and huge cold air mass produces a weather system. The warm air rises over the cold air and the cold air is sucked in underneath the warm air. This creates a warm front that is followed by a cold front. The two fronts begin to rotate, following each other. Eventually a swirling weather system results, with bands of cloud along the fronts. The rising warm air creates low pressure, so the system is called a low-pressure system. Air flows into the weather system from outside, following a spiral course, creating strong winds. There are also high-pressure systems called anticyclones, formed where air rotates as it sinks towards the surface.

Extreme fronts

If there is a wide temperature difference between the two air masses that form a front, extreme weather can result. At a cold front, towering cumulonimbus clouds form, with thunder and lightning, extremely heavy rain, hail, heavy snowfall or freezing rain, and even tornadoes (see page 17).

▶ A low-pressure weather system seen from space. Winds are swirling into the centre, where the air pressure is lowest.

TROPICAL STORMS

A tropical storm is a swirling weather system that begins life in the tropics. The most powerful tropical storms are called hurricanes, typhoons or cyclones, depending on where in the world they form. The weather inside hurricanes is much more severe than that inside the low-pressure systems that form at weather fronts (see page 12).

STORM FORMATION

The tropical seas are heated intensely by the Sun, causing rapid evaporation and rising air currents. Large cumulus clouds form, which often develop into groups of thunderstorms. In some cases these thunderstorms begin to spin, forming a swirling tropical storm. If a tropical storm moves across more warm water, it grows larger and more intense. If the wind speeds inside become greater than 119 km/h the storm is classified as a hurricane. A hurricane can grow to be hundreds of kilometres across and many kilometres high. Inside the hurricane are bands of thick cloud, and at the centre is a hole, called the eye,

▲ This view from space on 5 September 2004 shows Hurricane Ivan, a category 5 hurricane, which caused extensive damage in the Caribbean and the southern USA.

surrounded by a wall of cloud. The strongest winds blow inside this wall, but it is almost calm in the eye. Hurricanes can travel for thousands of kilometres, always moving westwards and curving away from the equator. They lose strength when they move over land.

HURRICANE EFFECTS

The intensity of a hurricane is given on a scale of 1 to 5, with category 5 being the most powerful (with wind speeds greater than 248 km/h). Any hurricane of category 3 or above is extremely destructive when it hits land, bringing damaging winds and intensely heavy rain. However, the most dangerous effect of a hurricane is called a storm surge. The very low air pressure inside a hurricane allows the sea level to rise at the centre of the hurricane, sometimes by several metres. When the hurricane hits land, this surge can cause serious flooding.

▲ In 2005, the storm surge caused by Hurricane Katrina flooded New Orleans, USA. Tragically, 1,836 people died.

Hurricane patterns

Hurricanes occur both in the northern hemisphere and the southern hemisphere. In the northern hemisphere, they always rotate anti-clockwise, and form between June and November. In the southern hemisphere they always rotate clockwise, and form between November and May. The months when they form are called hurricane seasons. There are about 20 category 4 or 5 hurricanes each year.

EXTREME WEATHER

Many areas of the world regularly experience extremes of weather. For example, the temperature becomes extremely low in the Arctic and Antarctic, and extremely high in some parts of the tropics. And there are powerful winds inside hurricanes and tornadoes. However, there can be extreme weather events in almost any place on Earth.

▲ Here, the top of a cumulonimubus cloud many kilometres high is spreading out, producing what is known as an 'anvil top' cloud.

STORM CLOUDS

Thunder and lightning are associated with towering clouds called cumulonimbus clouds. These clouds form where very humid air rises high into the atmosphere. They can be up to 10 km high, with flat tops that spread out into the lower stratosphere. Inside a cumulonimbus cloud are very powerful vertical air currents. The movement of ice crystals and water droplets in these currents causes static electricity to build up inside the cloud — negative charge at the top and positive charge at the bottom. When the charges become large enough, electricity jumps inside the cloud, from one cloud to another or to the ground. The flow of electricity heats the air suddenly, which causes the rumble of thunder. Thunder clouds produce intense rain and often hail.

Floods

Rivers flood when too much water flows down them to be contained by the banks. Floods are normally caused by continuous heavy rain over a long period, filling rivers to breaking point. Flash floods happen where extremely heavy rain falls in a small area. They create fast-flowing and destructive torrents of water.

▶ A flash flood tore through Boscastle, UK, in 2004.

Hailstones form when pieces of ice circulate up and down in a cloud, growing larger until they are heavy enough to fall.

THE HIGHEST WINDS

High winds are common on mountain tops and in low-pressure systems, but the strongest winds are in hurricanes and tornadoes. Hurricane winds can reach speeds of more than 250 km/h. The highest wind ever recorded was in a tornado, at 484 km/h. Tornadoes form under giant cumulonimbus clouds called super cells, which contain turbulent air currents. The currents cause the air inside a cloud to spin, and a rapidly spinning column of air called a vortex descends from the cloud to the ground. Air is sucked up the vortex, along with debris from the ground. Tornado Alley, in central USA, experiences the largest number of tornadoes each year. Here, cool polar air from Canada and warm tropical air from the Gulf of Mexico meet, setting off tornadoes.

▶ *The violent energy of a spinning tornado is captured in the dramatic picture.*

SEASONS

Most places on Earth have different weather at different times of year. The periods of different weather are called seasons. The changing seasons happen because of the way the Earth orbits the Sun. As it orbits the Sun, different areas of the Earth's surface are heated more or less at different times of year, affecting the weather and creating seasons.

THE TILTED EARTH

The Earth orbits the Sun once a year. As it orbits, it spins once every day on its axis. The axis is tilted over to one side, and this means that in different parts of the orbit, the same part of the Earth receives different amounts of heat from the Sun. When a part of the Earth is tilted towards the Sun, the Sun's rays hit the surface more straight on. The Sun appears high in the sky, and the heating effect is strong. When the same part of the Earth is tilted away from the Sun, the rays hit at a shallow angle. The Sun is low in the sky and the heating effect is weak.

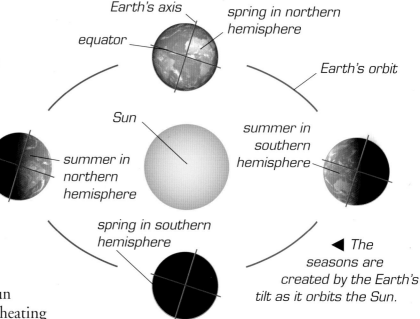

Earth's axis

equator

spring in northern hemisphere

Earth's orbit

Sun

summer in southern hemisphere

summer in northern hemisphere

spring in southern hemisphere

◄ The seasons are created by the Earth's tilt as it orbits the Sun.

FOUR SEASONS AND TWO SEASONS

The further north or south you go from the equator, the more the heating effect changes between one part of the year and another. Regions about halfway between the equator and the poles, or closer to the poles,

▶ *Seasons affect the look of the landscape. Here is the same location seen during spring (tl), summer (tr), autumn (bl) and winter (br).*

Monsoon seasons

In some parts of the world patterns of wind cause different weather at different times of year. The winds are known as monsoons. In India, monsoons bring dry and wet seasons. In winter, dry winds blow from north of the Himalayan mountains and down across India. They bring clear skies and dry weather. In summer, the wind reverses and blows north across India, bringing moist air and heavy rains in from the sea.

▼ *Pakistani commuters cross a flooded street after a heavy downpour in Karachi, 10 August 2007. Floods unleashed by a tropical cyclone and monsoon rains claimed over 200 lives.*

experience four seasons — winter, spring, summer and autumn. Autumn and winter happen in a place when it is tilted away from the Sun, and the days are shorter than the nights. Spring and summer happen when the place is tilted towards the Sun, and the days are longer than the nights. In the tropics there tend to be just two seasons — a wet season and a dry season. The wet season happens when a place it tilted towards the Sun, as the increased heat sets off evaporation and rainstorms.

RECORDING THE WEATHER

Meteorologists record the weather many times a day, every day, all year round. They record the temperature, the wind, rainfall and so on. These recordings are called observations.

Weather records allow us to compare the weather to the weather in the past, and to identify long-term changes. They also help with weather forecasting (see pages 22-23).

WEATHER STATIONS

A weather station is a collection of instruments used to measure the weather at a particular site. A station can be manual or automatic. At a manual station an observer reads

▼ *A typical manual weather station. The instruments are protected from the Sun, wind and rain by slatted wooden panels.*

▶ *An automatic, solar-powered weather station. Automatic stations are useful in remote areas.*

the instruments regularly (such as every three, six or twelve hours). At an automatic station, the instruments output digital data that is recorded. The data is sent by radio or cable to a meteorological centre.

There are thousands of weather stations dotted all over the Earth's surface, forming a vast global network of observation points. There are stations in city centres, along country roads, at schools, on remote mountain tops, on ships, oil rigs and weather buoys, and on aircraft. The massive amount of data from these weather stations is gathered by national and international weather organisations and stored on computer, ready for use.

MEASURING INSTRUMENTS

Here are the main weather observations taken and the instruments that record them. Some of the instruments are enclosed in a box to keep off sunlight and wind, which could affect the readings.

- **Temperature:** thermometer or maximum and minimum thermometer (which records the highest and lowest temperatures over a period of time)
- **Rainfall:** rain gauge
- **Wind speed:** anemometer
- **Wind direction:** wind vane
- **Air pressure:** barometer
- **Humidity:** hygrometer
- **Cloud cover:** manual observation
- **Sunshine:** sunshine recorder

Remote sensing

Observations are also made by remote sensing, which provides data that weather stations cannot. Radiosondes are carried up through the atmosphere by balloon. They carry packages of instruments that measure wind speed, wind direction, temperature and so on at different levels in the atmosphere. Weather satellites record land, sea and air temperatures, and humidity. Radar detects rainfall and measures wind speeds in distant clouds.

WEATHER FORECASTING

A weather forecast is a prediction of what the weather is going to be like in the future. Forecasts are normally worked out by national and international weather organisations.

For most people, forecasts are handy for planning activities and deciding what to wear to go out. But forecasts are much more important for other people, such as pilots and mariners.

COMPUTER PREDICTIONS

Making a weather forecast means predicting what will happen in the atmosphere over the following hours and days — where winds will blow, how clouds will form, and so on. The first thing that's needed is up-to-date data showing what's happening in the atmosphere. This is taken from the network of weather stations. The data is fed into computer programs that model the atmosphere. These are fantastically complicated, and need some of the world's most powerful computers to run them. The models perform billions of calculations to work out how the atmosphere is likely to change. Human input is still useful —

▼ *Meteorologists at this US weather centre rely on powerful computer modelling to make accurate predictions.*

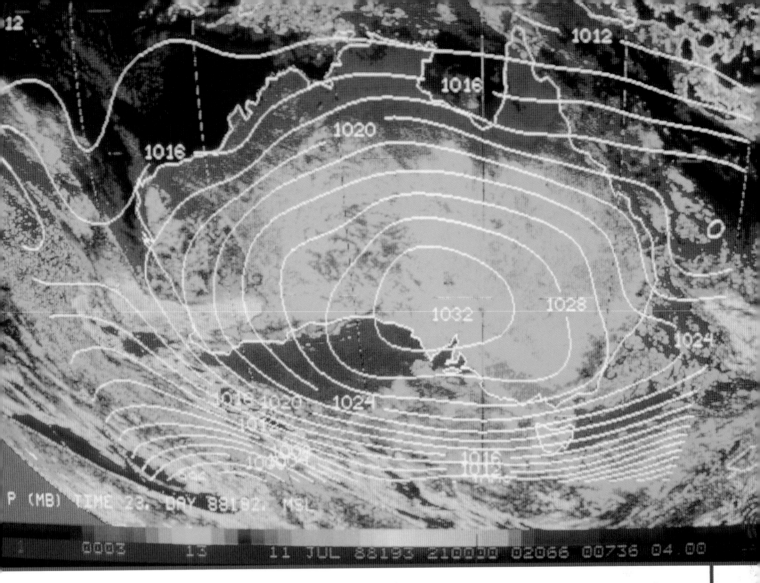

P (MB) TIME 23. DAY 88192 MSL

1 0003 13 11 JUL 88193 210000 02066 00736 04.00

experienced forecasters can predict local events such as thunderstorms that computer models cannot. Satellite photographs and rainfall radar readings help forecasters to check if the computer predictions are coming true.

PRESENTING A FORECAST

Most people get their weather forecasts from the television, a website or a newspaper. These forecasts include simple weather maps. Severe weather warnings are flashed up when extreme weather is likely to cause disruptions, such as road closures or floods, or be a danger to the public. Hurricane and tornado warnings are vital for safety. Pilots, mariners, mountaineers and others need a more specialised forecast, as high winds, fog and snow could endanger their lives.

▲ *A computer monitor displaying a map of Australia with air pressure readings, combined with atmospheric data relayed live from a weather satellite.*

Long-term forecasting

The weather is unpredictable. The further ahead that meteorologists try to forecast, the more difficult it is for them to be accurate. For example, a forecaster could be pretty confident in predicting that it will start to rain in a certain place four hours later. He or she could also be confident in predicting a period of rain in the afternoon two days later. But it would be almost impossible to predict rain at an exact time two days later.

CLIMATES

A climate is the pattern of weather a place has over a long period of time. Weather happens hour to hour and day to day, but climate happens over months and years. For example, a place may have a climate with a warm period in one part of the year. But, during this period, the weather may be hot on some days and cold on other days.

CLIMATE ZONES

There are many different climates around the world. Each area that experiences a different climate is called a climate zone. Reasons for different climate zones include heating by the Sun, closeness to the oceans, and height above sea level. In general, climates change from warm to cool as you move from the equator to the poles.

▲ *In tropical climates it is wet and warm all year – perfect weather for dense jungles to grow.*

CLIMATE ZONE EXAMPLES

There are many different ways of describing and naming the world's climate zones. See below for some of the most common climate zones. These are often further divided into smaller zones, such as sub-tropical and semi-arid. Climates are often summarised with temperature and rainfall charts, as presented here for London (temperate) and Mangalore (monsoon tropical). These show the average temperature and rainfall at a place over a year.

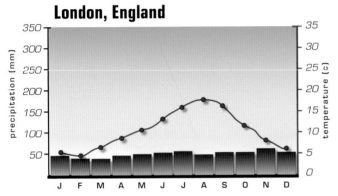

London, England

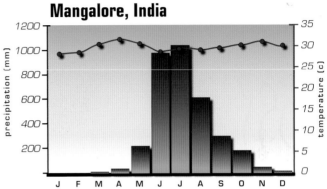

Mangalore, India

Tropical Here, the weather is warm and humid all year round. It is wet most of the year, except for a short dry season.

Arid Here, it is dry all year round. The days are hot and the nights are cold. The winter is colder than the summer.

Mediterranean Here, there are four seasons, but with hot, dry summers and cool, wet winters.

Temperate Here, there are four seasons — a warm summer, autumn, a cold winter, and spring. There is some rainfall all year round.

Polar Here, there are long, very cold winters, and short, cool summers. Snow can fall at any time of the year.

Mountain Here, it is colder, wetter and windier than on the surrounding plains, often with snowfall.

Microclimates

A microclimate is a climate that happens in one small area. Microclimates normally happen because of the local geography of the area. For example, valleys on one side of a mountain range are often drier than valleys on the other side, and coasts normally have less cold winters and less hot summers than places inland. The side of a valley that faces the Sun (eg south-facing in the southern hemisphere) often has a warmer, drier climate than the opposite side.

Cities often have slightly warmer climates than the surrounding countryside. In the city, the temperature can be one or two degrees Celsius higher than the surrounding countryside. This effect is known as an urban heat island. Reasons for it are waste heat energy from buildings and vehicles, buildings preventing heat loss from the ground at night, glass-covered buildings trapping heat in the streets, and the lack of vegetation, which would otherwise help to cool the air.

ADAPTING TO CLIMATES

Animals and plants live on almost every part of our planet, from hot, dry deserts to freezing mountain tops. Some inhabit places where it is hard to imagine they could survive. But they do survive because they are adapted to live in these climatic conditions.

ANIMAL ADAPTATIONS

In polar climates, animals must prevent heat loss from their bodies as much as possible. They do this with thick fur, feathers or layers of fat under the skin. In temperate climates, animals must survive through winters without much food. Some cope by hibernating in the winter months. They go into a deep sleep and lower their heart rates to conserve energy. Other animals, mostly birds, migrate to places with warmer climates during winter. In arid climates, where it is hot and dry, many animals stay underground in the heat of the day. Small animals can live without drinking water — they get all they need from the food they eat.

▲ *Polar bears are well adapted to the severe cold of the Arctic. They are insulated by thick fur and a 10-cm layer of blubber under their skin.*

PLANT ADAPTATIONS

In polar climates and mountain climates, plants such as lichens cling to rocks and grow only in summer, and trees and shrubs grow close to the ground to avoid damage from strong winds. In temperate climates, deciduous trees lose their leaves in autumn and winter to save energy and water. Conifer trees have needles instead of leaves, that don't freeze in winter. In arid climates, plants must avoid losing any precious water. Their long roots soak up water after rainfall, and their leaves are waxy to stop them drying out. Other plants that live in arid climates come to life only in the rainy season.

▲ *Cacti plants are adapted to living in very hot and dry conditions. They have thick stems that store water, and tiny leaves to reduce water loss.*

Humans and climates

Humans live almost everywhere on the planet, as do plants and other animals. We have found ways of coping with extremes of weather in the different climates. For example, in very hot, arid climates, people generally wear loose-fitting clothes, and live in homes with thick walls that keep the inside cool.

▼ *These mud-brick buildings in the Wadi Doan Valley, Yemen are built with thick walls to keep the inhabitants cool even in the hottest weather.*

CLIMATE CHANGE

Evidence from around the world shows that the overall temperature of the Earth's atmosphere is slowly rising. This is known as global warming. In turn, global warming is making the world's climates change. Most scientists agree that human activities are causing climate change.

THE GREENHOUSE EFFECT AND GLOBAL WARMING

Certain gases in the atmosphere trap heat from the Sun. This is called the greenhouse effect. The main 'greenhouse gas' is carbon dioxide. The amount of carbon dioxide in the atmosphere is rising, so that more and more heat is being trapped. Methane is another greenhouse gas. The carbon dioxide being added to the atmosphere comes from burning fossil fuels in vehicle engines and power stations, and for heating and cooking. It also comes from deforestation. Methane comes from cattle and rice farming.

▼ Destruction of the rainforests releases carbon dioxide into the atmosphere, and prevents the trees from soaking it up.

FIGHTING GLOBAL WARMING

The Intergovernmental Panel on Climate Change (IPCC) produces reports on climate change. It says that carbon-dioxide emissions must be cut radically over the next decade if we are to stop global warming. Negotiations are going on between countries to agree cuts in carbon dioxide emissions, but there are many hurdles to overcome, as countries such as India and China want to develop their industries. Ways of cutting emissions include using more energy from renewable sources, using less energy overall, and stopping deforestation. We must take action now to fight global warming. But whatever we do, some climate change is going to happen, and this will create more frequent extreme (and damaging) weather events. So we must also prepare for changes in the weather, and be ready to adapt when they happen.

▲ *Retreating glaciers are evidence for global warming. The sign marks where the glacier used to be in 1978.*

Climates in the past

Climates have been changing throughout the history of the Earth. For example, 1,000 years ago climates were a little warmer than today, but 50,000 years ago they were much colder. We know about these changes from studying growth rings in ancient trees, trapped bubbles of air in very old ice, old weather records and other evidence.

GLOSSARY

air pressure the push made by the air on everything in it

atmosphere the layer of air that surrounds the Earth

atmospheric pressure see air pressure

barometer an instrument that measures air pressure

climate the pattern of weather that a place experiences over a long period of time

climate change the slow changes in climate that are happening because of global warming

deforestation the gradual loss of the world's forests because of land clearances and logging

equator the imaginary line around the middle of the Earth, halfway between the poles

evaporation the change of state of a material from liquid to gas, normally below the material's boiling point

glacier a slow-moving river of ice that flows down from a mountain range

greenhouse effect the process that traps heat from the Sun in the atmosphere

growth rings a series of rings visible on the top of a tree stump, formed by faster and slower growth of the tree in past summers and winters

meteorologist a scientist who studies the weather

meteorology the science of the weather

northern hemisphere the half of the Earth to the north of the equator

pressure see air pressure

satellite a spacecraft that moves around the Earth in space

sea level the average level of the surface of the water in the sea

southern hemisphere the half of the Earth to the south of the equator

tropics the region of the Earth's surface around the equator, between the tropics of Cancer and Capricorn

turbulent describes movement that is not smooth, but rough and random

water vapour the gas form of water

Further information

The Meteorological Office
Home page of the UK's Meteorological Office. Includes pages on weather and climate for students.
www.metoffice.gov.uk/

NASA
Lots of amazing photographs of hurricanes taken from space.
www.msfc.nasa.gov/news/camex/camphotos.html

US National Weather Service
Home page of the US National Oceanic and Atmospheric Administration's National Weather Service. Includes a hurricane and tornado warning service.
www.nws.noaa.gov/

US National Severe Storms Laboratory
Lots of information on tornadoes and other severe weather in the USA.
www.nssl.noaa.gov/

University of California
An animated water cycle diagram from the University of California.
http://earthguide.xucsd.edu/earthguide/diagrams/watercycle/index.html

World Meteorological Organization
Home page of the World Meteorological Organization. Lots of useful information about the weather.
www.wmo.int/pages/index_en.html

NOTE TO PARENTS AND TEACHERS:
Every effort has been made by the Publishers to ensure that the websites in this book are suitable for children, that they are of the highest educational value, and that they contain no inappropriate or offensive material. However, because of the nature of the Internet, it is impossible to guarantee that the contents of these sites will not be altered. We strongly advise that Internet access is supervised by a responsible adult.

INDEX